THE POWER OF
A GUILT-FREE LIFE

SILENCING THE ACCUSER

GREGORY DICKOW

Silencing the Accuser:
The Power of a Guilt-Free Life
©2018 by Gregory Dickow Ministries.

All rights reserved.

No part of this book may be used or reproduced in any manner whatsoever—graphic, electronic, or mechanical—without written permission, except in the case of reprints in the context of reviews.

Printed in the United States of America

For information, please write:
Gregory Dickow Ministries
P.O. Box 7000
Chicago, IL 60680

You can visit us online at:
www.gregorydickow.com

ISBN 13: 978-1-932833-30-0

Second Printing, 2021

GREGORY **DICKOW**

@gregorydickow

gregorydickow.com

TABLE OF CONTENTS

Chapter One: No Record Against Us!........................... 5

Chapter Two: Use Your Imagination........................... 11

Chapter Three: Sinners by Birth 15

Chapter Four: Righteous by Re-Birth......................... 19

Chapter Five: Silencing the Accuser.......................... 23

Chapter Six: Breaking Free from Condemnation............... 29

Chapter Seven: Embrace the Gift of Forgiveness.............. 35

Chapter Eight: The Gateway to Power......................... 37

Chapter Nine: Jesus is Your Lawyer, Judge, & Jury 41

Chapter Ten: Jesus Saves Us from Sin........................ 45

Chapter Eleven: Putting an End to Guilt Forever 49

Chapter Twelve: I Find No Fault in Him...................... 55

Chapter Thirteen: Location, Location, Location 61

Chapter Fourteen: Who Will Bring a Charge Against God's Elect?....... 67

Chapter Fifteen: Feeling Free!............................... 71

The Gift of Salvation 75

As You Go Forward... 79

NO RECORD AGAINST US!

Chapter One

There's a story of a man in England who, years ago, had purchased the most expensive car in the world, a Rolls-Royce. He decided to take a vacation to France, and he wanted to take his Rolls-Royce with him to tour through the French countryside. So he put the Rolls-Royce on a ferry and went across the English Channel. As he was enjoying the French Riviera, suddenly his Rolls-Royce broke down, and there was nobody there who could fix this unique and complicated engine. He contacted the company headquarters in England, and they flew a man over immediately, who performed the repairs. He knew the repairs would be expensive, but it had to be done.

To this man's surprise, when he returned to London, he never received a bill for the repairs. In fact, they never sent a bill. So he sent a letter to the company communicating what had happened—how the mechanic had come over from England, fixed the car, and was still wondering what the charge would be. He got a letter back from the Rolls-Royce Company, saying as follows, "Dear Sir, thank you so much for your letter. You need to know that we have NO RECORD in our files that any Rolls-Royce has EVER broken down at ANY place, at ANY time, and for ANY reason. Therefore, you owe us nothing and never will." **This story really spoke to me: No matter what is broken in our lives, no matter what we've done, no matter how many flaws we've had, our great Manufacturer—our Master Builder—forgives and fixes us by His grace, and declares that there is NO RECORD against us; there is no debt to be paid. We owe nothing for our sins, and we never will! Through the precious blood of Jesus, God declares us: NOT GUILTY!**

I love what Job says in Job 10:7, *"According to YOUR knowledge I am indeed NOT guilty"* (NASB).

Notice, he says: ***according to God's knowledge***—as far as He is concerned, we are NOT guilty.

According to our sins, mistakes, shortcomings, failures, and even according to our own opinion, and that of others, we ARE guilty. But, according to God's knowledge—we can live a life free from guilt, condemnation, and the misery that accompanies these negative emotions.

"In Him we have redemption through His blood, the forgiveness of our trespasses, according to the riches of His grace" (Ephesians 1:7, NASB).

I am convinced that multitudes of believers are suffering from a sickness that eats them up inside—a sickness called GUILT. Guilt is that horrible feeling inside when you do something wrong or fail to do something that you feel you should have done, and you feel terrible about it. Maybe you're struggling right now. Maybe a lie you told caused a lot of pain, and you feel tremendous guilt over it. Or you're struggling because of a sexual sin from your recent or distant past. Maybe it was last week, last month, or even 20 years ago. Maybe the enemy condemns you about a divorce, or a selfish mistake you made during your marriage. Perhaps it even destroyed your relationship or it's simply destroying you inside. Maybe you feel the burden of guilt for something that was done TO you. Perhaps you were abused and the enemy bombards YOU with the shame and guilt of it. And you carry that guilt and shame everywhere you go.

Nothing seems to rob us of our true vitality and purpose—our true joy and rest—more than guilt.

We feel the guilt of what we have done, what others have done to us, or not having done what we should have done . . .

As Paul wrote in Romans 7:19, *"For I do not do the good I want, but the evil I do not want is what I keep on doing"* (ESV).

Guilt causes us to continue our wrong behavior. Guilt causes us to make bad decisions. Guilt causes us to get angry and be harsh (to deflect our guilt). Guilt causes us to feel unworthy of blessing or opportunity. Guilt causes us to make promises to God we can't keep. Guilt makes us judgmental, drains us of strength, makes us feel low about ourselves.

Everyone needs to feel relieved of guilt—so we either temporarily cover guilt with excuses OR we experience the depths of God's grace and are completely liberated from guilt forever. And THAT is what I believe this book is going to help you experience.

USE YOUR IMAGINATION

Chapter Two

Imagine for a moment, what it would be like to feel totally free from guilt...

You would be able to handle mistakes and weaknesses or criticisms and critiques without crumbling or being defensive.

You would stop beating yourself up, to pay for your guilt.

You would have more energy, because guilt sucks the life out of you and the joy out of life.

You wouldn't be manipulated by others through guilt manipulation, and you wouldn't use it against others.

You would forgive freely because you'd realize you were forgiven freely.

And here's my all-time favorite: A life free from guilt will help FREE YOU FROM DEPRESSION.

Guilty feelings are the "building blocks" of depression. For many people, depression is self-inflicted punishment. They actually think to themselves: "I will make myself feel bad to pay for what I've done."

We get angry about 20 times a day. It's usually anger at ourselves, for an inner guilt or frustration with our personal disappointments. If we believe our anger is bad, we keep it inside. It takes so much energy to keep the anger bottled up that we get drained and worn out from all that effort. And, since we are not using our energy to fulfill our purpose and go after the good things God has for us, we miss out on many things and much happiness. The weariness and the losses add up to make us feel hopeless, lethargic, irritable, and sad. This is depression.

We've all experienced or witnessed a child being yelled at by their parent: "You are BAD" or "shame on you." Even if they don't use these words, they often make a child feel guilt or shame. If the parent's guilt-trip "works," the child might cry or silently feel bad about herself, as guilt shapes her soul. Now the parent thinks that the guilt-trip worked because the child feels bad. But it hasn't. The child doesn't learn to do good; they've just learned to feel bad until they stop getting punished. When the parent stops the punishment, the child may feel like "feeling bad" is what rescued her; thus starting a cycle of coping through guilt, yet staying in bondage within.

That is certainly not meant to be the catch-all explanation to all depression; but it is something we have all witnessed or experienced.

Guilt is a terrible master.

But, Paul went on to show us **the secret to living free from guilt and condemnation is not by feeling bad, but by embracing our new identity in Christ.**

"There is therefore NOW no condemnation for those who are IN CHRIST, who walk not after the flesh but according to the spirit" **(Romans 8:1). We'll visit the idea of being "in Christ" later, but notice this one concept:**

The spirit is: what agrees with what Jesus has done.

The flesh is: what doesn't agree with what Jesus has done.

Freedom from guilt, shame, and condemnation begins with the acceptance of what Jesus has done for us and who we are in Him—forgiven, redeemed, and free.

But there is an accuser, who is working overtime to accuse and condemn us continually. We will overcome his accusations of guilt and condemnation in a couple chapters, but first, we need to establish a couple things that will help put things in perspective.

SINNERS BY BIRTH

Chapter Three

I love this verse in John 1:29, John the Baptist sees Jesus coming to him and says, *"Behold the Lamb of God who takes away the sin of the world."* Look at the emphasis that is made here. The Bible doesn't say, "the Lamb of God who takes away the 'SINS' of the world"—plural, that is—although, Jesus certainly takes away all of our sins. But rather, the emphasis is on the root of the problem—the Lamb of God takes away the "SIN" of the world. The "sin" of the world was not your sin or mine. Our "sins" were the fruit of the problem, not the root. The "sin" of the world was Adam's sin. Because of one man's sin, we all were made sinners. (Romans 5:19) You didn't become a sinner because of your sin. You became a sinner by birth. You were born into sin, because you were a descendent of Adam. Adam took sin upon himself when he first sinned, and as a result, everybody that was born took on his spiritual DNA, which was the DNA of sin. What we have to realize is that it's not our sin that made us sinners. It's Adam's sin that made us sinners.

In fact, you can't do anything to become a sinner. You might not be as bad as Adolf Hitler, but you may not be as good as Mother Teresa. It doesn't matter. We all fall somewhere in between, hopefully closer to Mother Teresa! But, none of us are sinners because of our sin. We are sinners because of Adam's sin.

You didn't mount up a bunch of sins and then all of a sudden God called you a sinner. You were a sinner without mounting up one sin. You would have gone to hell if you lived a nearly perfect life. You may be thinking, "Why is that so important?" Here's why: when we realize that it wasn't our sin that made us sinners, then we'll also realize that it's not our righteousness that makes us righteous.

RIGHTEOUS BY RE-BIRTH

Chapter Four

One of my favorite scriptures is in Romans 5:19 where he says, *"Through one man's disobedience we were all made sinners."* Who was that one man? It was Adam, right? Through Adam's disobedience, every one of us became sinners.

But the scripture doesn't stop there in Romans 5:19. It also says, *"Through one man's obedience we have all been made righteous."* It was Adam's sin that made you and I a sinner. It was Jesus Christ's righteousness that made you and I righteous! So you can't do anything to become righteous.

The big deal is that you and I had nothing to do with being sinners the first time we were born, and you and I have nothing to do with being righteous when we're born again.

You are now the righteousness of God not because you do right things—just like you weren't a sinner because you did wrong things; you're not righteous because you do right things. You're righteous because you were born-again righteous (in right standing with God, with God-given rights to the promises and power of God). That's who you are! So now the objective is not trying to get all the sin out of our life. The objective is to realize who we really are. Say this: "I'm not a sinner anymore. I am the righteousness of God. I am forgiven. I am a child of God. I am now right with God. I now have a new nature. It's not natural for me to sin anymore. Now it's natural for me to do what's right." There is no greater freedom and liberty in life than to know who you really are.

You see, the word "sin" means: "to miss the mark, to miss the true end and 'scope' of our lives." Jesus doesn't just save us from our sins and sinful actions; He saves us from missing the true purpose and the true scope of our lives. God wants us to look through His 'scope.' He wants us to look at ourselves the way He looks at us—and the way He looks at us is the same way that He looks at Jesus. When He sees you, He doesn't see you as a sinner. He sees you as His precious, holy, and victorious child! He sees you as the righteousness of God. We have to get His "scope" and look at things through His eyes.

We can't just try to change our behavior without changing the way we think and without realizing who we now really are: the righteousness of God. Does that mean that we'll never sin again? No. We probably will sin again. We won't be sin-less. But when we realize that we are no longer sinners, and are free from the guilt of our sin, we will sin less. Get it? Now I want to show you how! But, it starts with identifying how the enemy works to undermine our righteousness and accuse us with guilt and condemnation. Time to throw down the accuser now . .

SILENCING THE ACCUSER

Chapter Five

"... 'Now salvation and strength and the Kingdom of our God, and the power of His Christ have come, for the accuser of our brethren, **who accused them before our God day and night**, has been cast down'" (Revelation 12:10).

One translation of this verse says, the accuser *"has been thrown down and hurled down."*

Being accused continually is what many of us have experienced because the enemy is "the accuser." In fact, the word 'devil' comes from the Greek word "diabolo." And everybody who understands a little spanish knows that 'devil' is translated as "diablo." (Maybe you even have a tattoo that says that on your body somewhere! Haha!) This word, "diabolo" comes from two words: "dia"—which means to penetrate and to "enter into"; we get the word diameter from this word "dia," which means to penetrate. And the word "ballo"—which is where we get the word "ball" from—to throw a ball—and it means: to throw at or to throw something at (in this case, accusations). So when you put these two words together ("dia" and "ballo") we get our meaning: to throw accusations at until they penetrate. So this is how the devil operates: He throws accusations at you day and night, day and night, etc . . . until he penetrates your soul, and there he releases explosive power through guilt, condemnation, and shame. And so if we can deal with guilt the way Jesus intended us to, by taking these accusations captive and learning how to overcome the accuser, we'll experience real freedom and joy.

But, we all know what it sounds like to be accused with guilt and condemnation. The voice of accusation becomes so familiar to us that it actually sounds like we're saying it to ourselves and it sounds like our voice. Thoughts like: "You never do enough. You don't say the right things. You don't measure up. You don't get it all done. You don't do enough for your children, for your parents, or for others. You don't do as much for others as they do for you. You always seem to blow it when you seem to be making progress. You say things you regret. You get angry too easily. You think bad thoughts. You don't have the right clothes. You eat too much. You don't exercise enough. You don't pray enough. You don't read enough. You don't serve enough." Sound familiar? And they stop coming in the form of: "YOU don't do enough." And they start coming in first-person form: "I don't do enough. I don't measure up. I don't have the right things. I'm not good enough. I say things I regret. I get angry easily, etc."

And as you begin to agree with these accusations, you are so weighed down with guilt that it brings you into a place of sadness and ineffectiveness in life. And if we could throw down these accusations of guilt once and for all, we could experience real freedom (the freedom Jesus paid for us to have) and we could experience a peace that passes understanding and a joy unspeakable and full of glory—that's the life that God has for you!

Back to Revelation 12:10, where it says, *"The accuser has been thrown down."*

And then it tells us how has he been thrown down. "And they overcame him by the blood of the Lamb and by the word of their testimony. And they were not in love with their lives, unto death."

Here are the 3 things that empower us to throw down the accusations of guilt, condemnation, and shame.

1. **The blood of the Lamb.** Jesus' blood not only cleanses us from all sin, but also cleanses us from guilt.

"Let us draw near with a sincere heart in full assurance of faith, having our hearts sprinkled from an evil conscience, and our bodies washed with pure water" (Hebrews 10:22).

And back in verse 19, it says, *". . . We draw near BY THE BLOOD OF JESUS."*

So notice what the blood of Jesus does: brings us into God's presence; gives us a sincere heart; GIVES US FULL ASSURANCE OF FAITH (God will do what He says because the blood of Jesus guarantees the promises of God); and OUR HEARTS ARE CLEANSED FROM AN EVIL GUILTY CONSCIENCE.

2. **The word of our testimony.** We silence the accuser through our words! As we declare what Jesus has already done (saved us, forgiven us, healed us, redeemed us, loved us, made us kings and priests, etc.), the accuser is thrown down!

3. **And loving not our lives** . . . While this speaks of their willingness to lay down their lives, it also speaks to what they truly loved: They were in love with the life of Jesus, not their former lives. They were in love with who they were in Christ, not who they were in their former life or reputations. We must love finding our identity in Christ. And love the NEW YOU that God made you to be. This is how they were able to throw down the accuser of the brethren. Jesus threw him down and now we must continue to remind him that he's down. And refuse to let him back into our thinking!

Remind yourself of what the blood of Jesus has done for you. Speak and declare the testimonies of what He's done, and love the life Jesus has created in you—the new you.

This puts the enemy on the run and silences him from accusing you in your mind!

It's time to stop beating yourself up about your mistakes, about your past, about what you've done, or about what others have done to you.

Because we're so accustomed to feeling guilty and knowing how flawed we are, we allow guilt to control us. And we allow guilt to influence our decisions so that we can feel like we've paid for our guilt. But, we don't have to pay a cent for our guilt because Jesus already paid for it in its entirety, so that now we can live a guilt-free life. No matter what you feel like, no matter how many mistakes you've made, no matter how far you've fallen short, you can live a life where you're not guilty. And by the way, when you live a life of freedom from guilt, you're going to be able to pray with power, because what keeps us from being able to pray with authority and power is condemnation.

BREAKING FREE FROM CONDEMNATION

Chapter Six

"If our heart condemns us, God is greater than our heart and knows all things. But if our heart does not condemn us, then we have confidence towards God..." (1 John 3:20-21). Listen to what He says, *"Beloved, if our heart does not condemn us, then we have confidence before God."* So when you go to God in prayer, *"Then we can ask anything, and whatever we ask, we receive from Him"* (verse 22).

But go back to verse 21, where he says, *"If our heart does not condemn us, then we have confidence before God."* So what is he saying? When your heart condemns you, you don't have confidence before God, and you can't ask and receive because you lack confidence. And why are you lacking confidence? Because condemnation robs you of confidence. Sin does not rob you of confidence; the condemnation about it does. Mistakes don't rob you of confidence if you understand you're the righteousness of God, but the condemnation of those mistakes tries to rob us of confidence. Now I know that there is some incorrect religious thinking that has plagued our culture and plagued Christians and churches for years that says, "Well no, you can't say that, because it's sin that robs us of confidence." Really? Because if that's the case, then none of us could ever pray, because all of us have sinned; none of us could ever have confidence because all of us have sinned. He doesn't say, "If you have never sinned, then you can have confidence towards God." (I'm not encouraging you to sin. You understand!)

But he's not saying, "If you don't sin, then you can have confidence towards God." He's saying, "If your heart doesn't condemn you, then you have confidence towards God." Because even if we fall, even if we fail, and even if we stumble, our confidence doesn't come from our holiness. We can have confidence today because God is greater than our heart, making us the righteousness of God (in Christ). That's what gives us confidence. And if I fall or stumble, it doesn't change the fact that I'm the righteousness of God. But religious error has tried to confine us to be a byproduct of our behavior. And God wants us to understand it's the opposite. Our behavior is a byproduct of what we believe. Believe right = live right. Living right is the reflex of believing right.

But here is why we need to be delivered from guilt and condemnation through the blood of Jesus: because when we are not condemned, we have confidence before God. And if we have confidence before God, what's the effect? Verse 22: *"and whatsoever we ask we receive from Him."* When we have confidence, we will receive whatever we ask of Him! We will not receive from God if we do not have confidence before

God and we will not have confidence before God if our heart is condemned. And our heart can only be free from condemnation through the blood of Jesus. There is NO condemnation for those who are in Christ!

Now, back to Revelation 12:10, which talks about the accuser of the brethren . . . Satan wants to accuse you continually. Satan wants to make you feel bad continually. And we make bad decisions when we feel bad. We've got to stop making decisions to alleviate our guilt.

It reminds me of the guy who wrote to the IRS:

> "Dear IRS, enclosed you will find my money order for $150. You see, I cheated on my income tax return last year and have not been able to sleep ever since.
>
> If I still have trouble sleeping, I will send you the rest of what I owe you.
>
> Sincerely,
>
> A Taxpayer . . ."

And it's funny how this guy, as much of a joke as that is, only paid his taxes because he felt guilty. He felt bad and gave only to the degree that it would get his guilt to go away.

We've got to stop giving out of guilt, doing better out of guilt, praying out of guilt, repenting out of guilt, or confessing out of guilt. Guilt is not what frees us; guilt imprisons us. Jesus does not want you operating from a mindset of guilt. Now you say, "Well, doesn't a person have to feel guilty in order to change? Doesn't a person have to feel guilty in order to repent?" No, the Bible says in Romans 2:4, *"It is the lovingkindness of God that leads us to repentance,"* not guilt. Nowhere does the Bible say *guilt makes you repent*. Nowhere does it say *guilt makes you change.* However, guilt imprisons you.

In fact, guilt and feeling bad (feeling accused) all the time is a force from hell; it's from the accuser of the brethren. God doesn't use the devil. God does not employ the devil. God doesn't pay the devil. The devil is not on our team. Now, God can take what the devil has done and turn it into something good, but not because He employed the devil, and not because He dispatched the devil to do it. Even with Job, God didn't say, *"Ok Satan go ahead and smite Job."* He said, in essence: *"He's always been under your power. You have the power to do whatever you want to do to him."* Job wasn't under the new covenant blessing. The blood of Jesus had not yet been shed in the earth. So Satan had power to afflict Job's life. And it was Satan that attacked Job (Job 2:7). It was not God that said, *"Hey Satan, go do this for Me to teach Job a lesson."* Again, God doesn't employ the devil. He can transform what he's done to you and turn it into something good, but, God is not the accuser and does not use guilt to get you to change. He uses kindness, grace, and the power of the Holy Spirit.

We have to realize Jesus alleviates our guilt through His blood, through His precious, precious blood—not through our behavior, or through our feeling bad long enough.

EMBRACE THE GIFT OF FORGIVENESS

Chapter Seven

Embrace God's forgiveness right now and forgive yourself. It's so important to forgive yourself. You might think: "Oh, I can forgive others, but I could never forgive myself." But that's not true. If you can't forgive yourself, you can't forgive others, because you can only treat people the way you treat yourself. If you hate yourself, you will eventually hate other people. If you love yourself, with God's love, you'll eventually love other people. You will eventually reflect and project upon others what you feel about yourself, and that's why it's so essential that you forgive yourself if you've blown it. That's one of the things that cripples us.

We believe mentally that God has forgiven us. We believe even that other people have forgiven us, but our most difficult trial is forgiving ourselves. So, how do you forgive yourself? Well, how did God forgive you? Did He forgive you because you felt bad enough? No. Did He forgive you because you repented? No. He forgave you because He paid the price for that sin. So forgive yourself for the same reason: that God forgave you. He forgave you because He paid the price. Forgive yourself because He paid the price. When God forgave you, He forgave immediately; He forgave completely; He forgave freely. Think about how great His love is. He forgives immediately. He doesn't make you wallow in it for a while; even though we might try do that to other people, God doesn't do that to you or me. Thank God for that. He forgave you immediately; He forgave you completely; and He forgave you freely.

THE GATEWAY TO POWER
Chapter Eight

Remember those four guys that brought their friend to Jesus' house and there was no room for them, so they went up on the roof, and lowered him down through the roof? The boy was paralyzed and Jesus looked at him and said, *"Son, your sins are forgiven you."* I used to wonder why Jesus said, "Your sins are forgiven," when what he really needed was healing. But Jesus is showing us the greatest need in all of our lives. No matter what the condition of life is, whether we're sick, whether we're diseased, whether we're poor, whether we're depressed or discouraged, or whether we are fighting through marriage, family, or emotional problems, the greatest need of every one of our lives first and foremost, is to know we are forgiven and to hear from the lips of the Savior Himself, *"My child, your sins are forgiven."* It was only then that He went back to that boy and said, *"Take up your bed and go home."* Because an unforgiven man doesn't feel worthy to receive healing, but a forgiven man knows that "if God could have mercy on me enough to forgive me for all that I've done wrong, He can certainly heal me from whatever is ailing me".

His faith got him up because he knew he was forgiven. When a woman was caught in adultery, Jesus didn't say, "Go and sin no more and THEN you'll be forgiven. Go and sin no more and

THEN I won't condemn you." No! No! No! A thousand times no! Jesus said, *"Who condemns you?"* She said, *"No one, Lord."* Jesus responded: *"Neither do I condemn you!"* Jesus was saying, "You've been guilty, but I declare you not guilty. You deserve to be condemned, but I declare I don't condemn you and I have the final word on the matter." Then He said, *". . . Now go and sin no more"* (John 8:11). FIRST, He alleviated her guilt and condemnation. He was saying: Now that you know you are forgiven, now that you know that you are not condemned, NOW you can GO and sin no more. The power to be healed, the power to break free from sin, addictions, habits, or bad behavior, is to KNOW THE POWER OF A GUILT-FREE HEART—to know you are forgiven!

JESUS IS YOUR LAWYER, JUDGE, & JURY

Chapter Nine

Satan is the accuser of the brethren who accuses day and night. The enemy brings the accusation, but Jesus is your defender! He is our lawyer, the judge, and the jury. He stands in the gap as our intercessor, swallows up all of the accusations, nails them to the cross, and says: *"Who will bring a charge against My elect? It is God who justifies"* (Romans 8:33).

The scripture goes on to say:

"Who is the one who condemns? Christ Jesus is He who died, yes, rather who was raised, who is at the right hand of God, who also intercedes for us" (Romans 8:34).

So what does it mean that Jesus is interceding for us? It means: He stands in between us and the accuser.

The devil is the accuser. We are the accused. Jesus is the judge, the lawyer, and the jury. He steps into this world. He absorbs the accusations on the cross and then presents the evidence of His blood, as our lawyer advocate. He decides along with the Father and the Holy Spirit, as the three-strand jury. And then declares that the price has been paid and He brings forth the judgment: "My son or daughter is forgiven. They are NOT GUILTY anymore."

Satan may be the accuser, but he is not the final judge! God has found us not guilty. It's not about proving that you're "a pretty good guy" or "a pretty good girl." It's not about proving that you're "not that bad." It's about laying it all on the table. The devil says, "There's the evidence. There's their sin, God. Look at all that they did. There's the proof that they're guilty." And Jesus steps in, lays His blood on that table and says, "No THERE'S the evidence. Look at all that I DID. There's the proof that they're NOT GUILTY." And want to know what happens when you know that you're not guilty? Satan has nothing on you. He's got no power to affect you. He's got no power to influence you. He can't bring sickness whenever he wants to bring it against you. He can't bring condemnation whenever he wants to bring it against you. He can't bring discouragement whenever he wants to bring it against you. He can only bring those things on the guilty.

I John 2:1 says that Jesus is our lawyer defending our cause, defending our case, saying about us and saying to us "not guilty." We might say: "No, Lord, I am guilty. I did this wrong." He says, "But I declare you're not guilty." We say, "But Lord, you know what I did." He says, "Not anymore. My blood has washed away any evidence. I say again, you are not guilty." We respond, "But Lord, I feel really bad and I need to feel bad a little bit longer and, you know, say a few prayers maybe and get this thing off of me." He responds, "No, all you have to say is: 'I accept Your verdict, Lord.'"

Growing up Catholic, I used to think, "I'll say a few 'Our Fathers' and throw in a few 'Hail Marys'. And I'll be forgiven." I didn't know that I couldn't absolve myself. I didn't know that I couldn't justify myself.

We don't need to fix ourselves. We need to receive what He's done for us and begin to think "not guilty." Does that mean you didn't do it? You did it, but the verdict in His blood prevails. It's not that we deny that we did it. It's that we receive His decree that we're not guilty.

JESUS SAVES US FROM SIN
Chapter Ten

I have found one of the most powerful verses in the whole Bible to be about the first coming of the Lord Jesus. We have to truly understand the first coming of the Lord Jesus Christ, so that we can prepare ourselves for His second coming. I believe this capsulizes the intention and purpose that God brought Jesus to this earth for.

In Matthew 1:21, it says, speaking of Mary, *"And she shall bring forth a son and you shall call His name Jesus for He shall save His people from their sins."* **He shall save His people from their sins.** I realize that maybe you've heard or read that verse many times, but many have failed to truly grasp the meaning of such a powerful and profound verse of scripture.

When it says, He shall SAVE His people from their sins, He's not just saying He shall FORGIVE His people for their sins. Forgiveness is one thing, but salvation from our sins is much greater. If we are born again, we are forgiven through the blood of Jesus. He forgives us. But to be saved from our sins is a much more complete truth that encompasses much more than just forgiveness. To be saved from our sins means that not only are we forgiven and not only is sin washed from us, but we are also DELIVERED from the power of that sin and delivered from the power of continuing in it!

"For sin shall not have dominion over you, for you are not under the law, but under grace" (Romans 6:14).

"And having been set free from sin, you have become slaves of righteousness" (Romans 6:18).

Let us put far more confidence in the blood-bought grace of Jesus—that it doesn't just deliver us from what we did wrong, but it delivers us from the consequences of it and delivers us from being under the dominion of it.

PUTTING AN END TO GUILT FOREVER

Chapter Eleven

Why do we feel guilty? Because of our past, because we make promises that we don't end up keeping, because we're not living up to our standards, because we're not living up to other's standards, we're not living up to God's standards. Or, we owe someone something that we can't pay, so we feel guilty. You know the best thing you can do, if you ever want to end a relationship? Loan somebody money! Because as soon as you loan it to them and they can't pay you back, they will disappear from your life! Haha!

But we feel guilty because we say something in anger that we later regret. We feel guilty about being overweight; we feel guilty when we look at the scale. I've got a simple solution for that: Get rid of your scale! ☺

We feel guilty because we don't finish our list, we're not spending enough time with our family, we're not praying enough, or reading our Bible enough. Or when we're reading our Bible, the devil is telling us we should be praying!

Or maybe you feel guilty because you have a messy house. Not doing enough for your family, not finishing what you started, or not helping more people, etc. Some of these things are simply normal and natural. And so we have to accept that we are humans. We have to accept that we are not flawless. We have to accept that we are going to make mistakes; we have shortcomings. It's not an excuse for them, but it's a reality that each and every one of us live in. And we can't be free from guilt by being perfect.

But we CAN be free! It starts right here in Hebrews 10:22, and I want to show you this verse from the New Living Translation:

"Let us go right into the presence of God with sincere hearts fully trusting Him. For our guilty consciences have been sprinkled with Christ's blood to make us clean, and our bodies have been washed with pure water."

Notice what he says, *"Our guilty consciences have been sprinkled with Christ's blood to make us clean."* He doesn't say our confession makes us clean. He doesn't say our apology makes us clean. He doesn't say that our holiness makes us clean. He doesn't say that our good works make us clean. I'm not saying that we should live unholy. I'm not saying that we shouldn't do good works. But none of those things cleanse us from a guilty conscience. He says only one thing cleanses us from a guilty conscience: the blood of Jesus Christ. He **sprinkles** us with His blood once and for all.

Now I don't know about you, but I'm into sprinklers that get the job done! How about you? Sometimes we think of "sprinkling us with His blood" like a light mist or an infant's baptism. The priest kind of dabs the baby's head with a few sprinkles of water. No!

By contrast, have you ever seen one of those sprinklers that can rip your feet right out from under you? There are some heavy-duty-golf-course sprinklers that are so powerful that they can peel the paint off the wall! And that's what I want you to envision with this verse. I don't want you to envision one of those fun summertime soft rainbow sprinklers that you used to jump in and out of as a kid. Those things could barely get you wet! No, we weren't cleansed with some "rainbow sprinkler"!

We were cleansed with the one that peels all the sin right off of us, and peels all the condemnation, all the guilt, all the shame, all your regrets, all of your mistakes, and all of your shortcomings off of you! And all that's left is you, washed by the blood of the Lamb, washed by the precious blood of Jesus, and no longer having to live with a guilty conscience ever again.

Whatever you've done . . . It's over. It's washed. You've been cleansed. I don't care what you say you've done, no matter how powerfully bad it is. "Oh, I cheated. I smoked. I drank. I lied. I did this; I did that." Let me encourage you—as bad as those things are, as powerful as those things are to condemn you forever, Jesus' blood is more powerful and it justifies you forever! It cleanses you forever and it makes you free from guilt forever.

Guilt just doesn't work and it doesn't lead us to freedom or change. It actually repels people from the gospel rather than drawing people to it.

A Christian lady told of a conversation she had with a fellow student while the two of them were studying in college at Berkeley University in California. She was a Christian but the guy she was talking to wasn't. And he made it painfully clear that he had no interest in her faith. When she asked, *"Why don't you want to become a Christian? Why don't you want to follow Jesus?"* He answered, *"Because the most guilt-ridden people I know are Christians; no thanks."*

Christians are unfortunately the best at feeling guilty and putting guilt on people. And we've got to stop it. We've got to stop feeling it. We've got to stop believing it and we've got to stop passing it on because the world is not going to come to Jesus because they feel guilty. They already feel guilty without Jesus. He didn't come to bring guilt. (John 3:17) He bore our guilt. He took our shame so that we would not have to be imprisoned by it any longer—held back by guilt. This guilt makes us prayerless, disheartened, and powerless.

Maybe you're struggling and you say, "Well, I can never get past this until I feel bad long enough." And you know what? There's only one person that could ever feel bad for what you've done and that's Jesus. He felt so bad, that He took it on the cross and nailed it to the cross. It does not honor God for you to live in guilt. It honors God for you to trade your guilt and shame for the gift of righteousness; that's what honors God. It honors God for you to believe in His powerful sprinkling blood.

I FIND NO FAULT IN HIM

Chapter Twelve

As we said earlier, nothing seems to rob us of our purpose more than guilt and shame. Nothing robs us of happiness and joy more than guilt and shame. We feel the guilt of what we've done and what others have done to us. Even if someone has been hurt or abused, they often feel guilty about that too. Whether it's someone else's fault or our fault, the enemy tries to condemn us. But, Jesus took all of our faults, all of our sins, all our guilt and shame, and nailed it all to the cross.

"*Pilate therefore went forth again, and saith unto them, Behold, I bring him forth to you, that ye may know that **I find no fault in him***" (John 19:4, KJV).

This scripture is amazing! I'll show you why in a minute. But look at it in another translation:

"*Pilate came out again and said to them, 'Behold, I am bringing Him out to you so that you may know that **I find no guilt in Him***'" (NASB).

So, when Pilate was sentencing Jesus, as the one in authority at that time, He was speaking prophetically over everyone who belongs to Christ! When he said, "I find no fault in Him," he was giving us a prophetic picture of how God sees us when we are born again.

You see, Pontius Pilate was in authority over that region of the world at the time, under Caesar; and the authority said, "I find no fault in Him." So this was a picture of what our authority—our Heavenly Father—says about us now that we are in Jesus Christ—who Pilate found no fault in! He took our faults and He took our sins, our guilt, our shame; and he that was in authority said, "I find no fault in Him," as a picture of how God, the ultimate authority, says about you and me, "I find no fault in them."

"For if that first covenant had been without fault, no place would have been sought for a second. But finding fault with the people, He said: 'Behold, the days are coming, says the Lord, when I will make a new covenant with the house of Israel and with the house of Judah'" (Hebrews 8:7-8).

You see, the problem with the Old Covenant, was not that it was incorrect. Everything in it is correct, and the inspired Word of God. BUT the problem with the Old Covenant, and the reason God made a New Covenant, is that the Old Covenant FOUND FAULT WITH US. The Old Covenant exposed our faults, but the New Covenant removes them!

The New Covenant, enacted by the blood of Jesus, finds no fault with us. The Spirit of Grace declares, *"And your sins and your iniquities, I will remember no more"* (Hebrews 8:12).

So if God doesn't remember them, why are we remembering them? Why are we reminding each other of them? Why are we reminding ourselves of them? Why are we letting the devil remind us of them when God doesn't even do so? He says in Hebrews 8:12, *"And your sins and your iniquities I will remember no more."* Now I don't know how else to get this across. I don't know how else to interpret this other than: He has "plum forgotten" all your unrighteousness, all your sins, all your lawless deeds, all your guilt, and all your fault. God has forgotten them all because they have all been stripped and washed away. If you strip paint off a wall that means that paint no longer exists. It's gone; it doesn't exist anymore. And that's what sin is in Christ; it doesn't exist anymore! You're no longer "in sin"; you're "in Christ," if you've been born again.

If we could rid ourselves of this guilt today, we would feel complete freedom from our past and freedom to walk in the joy and power of God. But we don't have to rid ourselves of it. Jesus already did. We simply need to agree with Him and accept this freedom. Identify only with our innocence, and with the blood of Jesus that washes us and makes us new. We've got to stop walking around guilty and weighed down with the depression of our past and our flaws.

But we all have struggled, just as Paul described. And God gives us a remedy:

"For I do not do the good that I want, but I end up doing the evil that I don't want to do; I keep on doing it" (Romans 7:19).

So what he's really talking about here is a "guilt sandwich." Here's what happens: When you don't do the good that you want to do, you feel guilty. And then when you feel guilty, you end up doing the evil that you don't want to do!

It's not that we do evil because we're evil. As believers, if we do evil, it's because evil is a by-product of guilt. And so if we can deal with guilt, the evil behavior will begin to diminish from our lives.

Let's see how this "guilt sandwich" works. We don't do what we want to do. We know the right thing to do, but we don't end up doing it, so we feel bad about not doing the right thing. And by feeling bad about not doing the right thing, we end up doing the wrong things. This is exactly what he's saying, and then he goes on to say in verse 24: *"Who will deliver me, wretched man that I am. Who will deliver me from this body of death?"*

And in verse 25, Paul tells us who will deliver him. He says, *"Thanks be to God through our Lord Jesus Christ!"*

He's saying only Jesus can deliver us. And watch how he does it: the very next verse is Romans 8:1 . . . *"There is therefore now no condemnation for those who are in Christ Jesus."* This is a continued thought from Romans 7:19, 24, and 25.

As we resist the condemnation, through our right-standing with God, the guilt disappears and we stop eating the sandwich!

The Lord spoke to me something recently about this verse: "Let me show you a secret to living in this freedom from condemnation. You simply have to understand your location!"

In real estate terms, the most valuable properties are defined by three words: "location, location, location." We have great value based on our location. We are "IN CHRIST" and there is no condemnation for those who are in Christ Jesus.

Forget about what you've done and realize WHERE you're located. You are in Christ Jesus. Stop worrying about where you've been or where you're trying to get to.

LOCATION, LOCATION, LOCATION

Chapter Thirteen

You know, when you go to the mall and you don't know where the store is that you're looking for, what do you do? You find the big directory map; and when you look at it, you're not even looking for the store! You know the first place you're looking for? You're looking for the little arrow that points and says: **You Are Here**. Because if you can discover WHERE you are, then it is easy to get to the destination. You know, those maps are so funny, yet frustrating, because all the stores are identified with small letters, in code, "39-A, 42-B," right? But the biggest thing on there is the little dot that says: **You Are Here**. Because frankly, there's nothing worse than a map that shows where everything is, but you don't know where you are, in respect to where everything else is. But once you know where you are, it puts everything in perspective. You know exactly how to get there. You know exactly where you're going. And what we need is . . .

We need a little map in our head telling us where we are: in Christ! We need that map reminding us continually, "You're in Christ; you're in Christ; you're in Christ."

Look at what it says in Ephesians 1:11, in the Message Bible, *"For it is in Christ . . ."* Where?

It is IN CHRIST, *"That we find out who we are and what we are living for."*

I want to show you three secrets in this chapter to breaking free from guilt. This is the **first secret** or key to getting out of this guilt trap: **location, location, location.** Where are you located? Where do you find yourself? Where are you? You are in Christ! And any other way of trying to find yourself will leave you miserable, lonely, sad, and without purpose or direction. Only *in Christ* will we find out who we are and what we're living for—nothing else and nobody else. Location, location, location: this is how to tear down that stronghold of guilt.

The **second way** to break free is that we must change the way we see ourselves. Notice what I didn't say. We don't need to change ourselves to stop feeling guilty. *We need to change how we see ourselves.*

You know, if you look in the mirror right now and look yourself in the eye, but you don't like the person that you're looking at, there's only one thing to do—forgive yourself. God made you to like yourself, but Satan's accusing you and trying to convince you that the shape of your ears have to change before you can be happy—or you have to stop getting angry to be happy or change some habit in order to stop the guilt to be happy. And it's all a lie. What you need to do is realize that there's something in you that feels guilty about what you've done or shame about who you are. And that's what's making you dislike yourself. It's not that you're not pretty enough or holy enough. Maybe you feel bad because you're comparing yourself to somebody else rather than looking at the person that God loves so much—He created you and died for you so that He could have a relationship with YOU! And if the Prince of the universe and the King of kings and Lord of lords wants to be with you, that means you are beautiful, valuable, and amazing to Him. And He doesn't want to ever miss out on having an intimate relationship with you. So you know what? You need to let go of guilt and forgive yourself so that you can start loving yourself the way God loves you.

And **thirdly**, we have to pull down the stronghold of guilt. What we have to realize is that guilt is often a greater sickness than physical disease at times. Remember when Jesus healed that boy we talked about earlier, when his friends brought him to the house because they couldn't get in? They lowered him through the roof; they put him in front of Jesus. And the first thing Jesus said was not "son, you're healed." He said, *"Son, your sins are forgiven you."* Your sins are forgiven! Why did He say, *"Your sins are forgiven"*? Because He knew that what would keep this guy in bondage, more than his paralysis, was guilt. And so He wanted to free him from guilt first. Receiving healing would be easy, if he could receive the forgiveness. Forgiveness from guilt is the gateway to all of God's power. See yourself forgiven and see yourself loved!

So, **number one**, we've got to know our location, location, location, is in Christ. And there's no condemnation for those that are in Christ.

Number two, we've got to change the way we see ourselves, love ourselves, and forgive ourselves.

And **number three**, we've got to pull down this stronghold of guilt, with God's Word. Let's do that now!

WHO WILL BRING A CHARGE AGAINST GOD'S ELECT?

Chapter Fourteen

Think about this verse in Romans 8:32. *"He who did not spare His own Son, but delivered Him up for us all, how shall He not also with Him freely give us all things?"* And I always wondered, why does the next verse say, *"Who will bring a charge against God's elect?"* Verse 32 is talking about all that God has given us, freely. With Jesus, He has given us all things, freely. What an awesome promise! He freely gave us Jesus. He freely gives us all things. But there's something in our heads, this guilt-ridden mentality, that says, "I don't deserve it." And yet it's free. "Oh, I haven't earned it." But, it's free! "I haven't done enough to get all these things." But, Jesus is telling us it's free. You don't have to do anything except receive it. But Satan is accusing you.

Every time God gives a promise, Satan gives an accusation. So God says, "Freely, He gives you all things," but your mind is being accused—"Well, you don't deserve it, you can't have it, you haven't done enough, look at what you've done, and look at how you failed." And so that's why the apostle Paul combats those inner conversations with the next verse.

"Who shall bring a charge (accusation) against God's elect? It is God who justifies. Who is the one that condemns? It is Christ Jesus who died and rose from the dead and is even sitting at the right hand of the Father, making intercession for you" (Romans 8:33-34).

No matter what you've done, no matter how much the devil tries to accuse you and tell you, "You don't deserve it. You're not worthy of God's blessing," God is showing us how to respond to that guilt. You say it: "Who will bring a charge against God's elect? It is God who justifies. Who is he that condemns?" That's why He says in verse 31, *"What shall we say to these things?"* We should say: *"There is therefore now no condemnation for those who are in Christ. Who shall separate us from the love of God?"*

What shall we say *to* these things? We should say: "Nothing can separate me from the love of God, in Christ. And nothing can condemn me and make me feel guilty another day of my life, unless I let it!"

These are the simple truths that will set us free from guilt and condemnation forever!

FEELING FREE!

Chapter Fifteen

So, what would it feel like to be free from guilt forever?

You will walk in the power of God!

You will feel the freedom to think big, dream big and ask big!

You will have confidence before God, so that whatever you ask, you'll receive from Him!

You will be happy, free, and become a magnet to others, drawing them to this freedom through the sheer joy that will flow from your heart.

You'll become the best version of yourself, because you'll be able to handle mistakes and weaknesses, and criticisms and critiques, without crumbling or being defensive.

You'll stop beating yourself up to pay for your guilt.

You'll have more energy, because guilt sucks the life out of you, and the joy out of life.

You won't be manipulated by others through guilt manipulation, and you won't use it against others.

You'll forgive freely because you realize you were forgiven freely!

You don't have to live in guilt another day of your life. Jesus has done all that is necessary, to declare you: Not guilty!

We don't have to spend another second feeling guilty because Jesus already paid for it in its entirety. From this day forward, we can live a guilt-free life.

Beginning today, decide to wake up in the morning and say: "Who shall bring a charge or accusation against me? NOBODY can, because it is Christ Jesus who justifies me. It is Christ Jesus who died, rose from dead, and is sitting at the right hand of the Father, having spilled His eternal blood, declaring me: NOT GUILTY! I am freely, completely, and eternally forgiven. I will walk in the power that comes from that forgiveness—the power to pray, the power to speak with authority, and the power to live in complete joy and freedom from this day forward."

"The steadfast love of the Lord never ceases; his mercies never come to an end; they are new every morning; great is Your faithfulness" (Lamentations 3:22-23).

No matter how bad your life has been, it's a new day! No matter how many things you've done wrong, it's a new day. You have a clean slate and a fresh start. Start believing this and peace will flow like a river!

Special Note: In each of my books, I desire to help lead people to the Lord—if they have never been born again, or are not certain of their salvation. Please use this for yourself or someone you know who may not know the Lord yet.

THE GIFT OF SALVATION

Your New Life Begins with God's Love

"This is the kind of love we are talking about—not that we once upon a time loved God—but that He loved us and sent His Son as a sacrifice to clear away our sins and the damage they've done to our relationship with God."

—1 John 4:10b MSG

Christianity is not a religion. It is a relationship between God and you.

God loves you deeply and wants a personal relationship with you! The Love of Jesus Christ will sweep away your sin, loneliness, pain, and fear. He wants you to spend eternity in Heaven with Him, and the rest of your life on this earth walking with Him. If you would like to begin a new life—beyond your wildest dreams and be born again—pray the following prayer, and believe in your heart that God answers!

"Heavenly Father, I believe that Jesus Christ died on the cross for my sins and rose from the dead. His blood washes away my past, my sins, and prepares me for eternity. I receive Your forgiveness and accept Jesus as my Savior and Lord. From this day forward, I am Yours, in Jesus' Name. Amen!"

If you have prayed this prayer, we would love to hear from you. Please call us at 847-645-9700, or simply email us at prayer@changinglives.org.

AS YOU GO FORWARD

Next Steps

As a believer, I encourage you to step out in faith and live every day as if it were your first day living for God. I also encourage you to do the following three things:

1. Read your Bible. The Bible has the answer to every problem that you could ever face. As you read and study, know that you have the same promises that God gave Abraham, David, and all of the great men and women in the Bible. You will find out exactly who you are and what you mean to Him. You will find out that He will never leave you or forsake you! You will be filled with strength and wisdom.

2. Get planted in church. By now, you understand the power that comes from the church family. You don't need to go to church to get into heaven, but you **DO** need to become equipped to fulfill God's will for your life. In Luke 4:16, we find it was Jesus' custom to go to church every week. If the Son of God made it His custom, how much more should we?

3. Tell somebody. One of the most rewarding things I have ever found in my life is the opportunity to share with others what God has done for me. You don't have to be a preacher. Just tell someone your simple story of God's love and plant the seed of the gospel in someone's life. You will be blessed, and so will they!

Well, what a journey you've just begun! And it is just that—a journey. Remember, the power of a new life is a process. It begins the moment you are born again, but it continues through our lives. We all face storms and trials, and we have an enemy, the devil, trying to stop our progress. But God has given us the tools and weapons to resist the enemy and be victorious in our journey. Build your life on these foundations and you will not fail!

"And the rain fell, and the floods came, and the winds blew and beat against that house; and yet it did not fall, for it had been founded on the rock" (Matthew 7:25).

**Gregory Dickow Ministries &
Life Changers International Church Mission Statement**

"Introducing people to the real Jesus;
empowering them to rise to their true worth
& purpose; and changing mind-sets
that change the world."

OTHER BOOKS AVAILABLE BY PASTOR GREGORY DICKOW

- Breaking the Power of Inferiority
- Fast From Wrong Thinking
- More Than Amazing Grace
- So Loved
- Taking Charge of Your Emotions
- The Power to Change Today
- Triumphing Over Loneliness
- Changed by Love

AUDIO SERIES AVAILABLE BY PASTOR GREGORY DICKOW

- Breaking the Power of Shame
- Command Your Day
- Fearless Living
- Healing the Father Fracture
- Identity
- Living in the State of Grace: Relocating to the Best Place on Earth
- From Stressed to Rest
- Mastering Your Emotions
- Radical Acceptance
- The End of Religion
- The Holy Spirit, Our Healer
- The Power of Emotional Intelligence

You can order these and many other life-changing materials by calling toll-free **1-888-438-5433**. For more information about Gregory Dickow Ministries, please visit **www.gregorydickow.com**.